THOMAS BREZINA

Tips & Tricks

FOR

Junior Detectives

Illustrated by Gabriele Klann & Bernard Forth

Sterling Publishing Co., Inc.
New York

Library of Congress Cataloging-in-Publication Data Available

Published by Sterling Publishing Company, Inc.
387 Park Avenue South, New York, N.Y. 10016

Originally published 1994 by hpt-Verlagsgesellschaft, Vienna (Austria)
under the title *Das Geheimbuch für Juniordetektive* © 1998 by
Ravensburger Buchverlag Otto Maier GmbH, Ravensburg (Germany)

English translation © 2000 by Sterling Publishing Co., Inc.

Distributed in Canada by Sterling Publishing
C/o Canadian Manda Group, One Atlantic Avenue, Suite 105
Toronto, Ontario, Canada M6K 3E7

Distributed in Great Britain and Europe by Chris Lloyd
463 Ashley Road, Parkstone, Poole, Dorset, BH14 0AX, England

Distributed in Australia by Capricorn Link (Australia) Pty Ltd.
P.O. Box 6651, Baulkham Hillls, Business Centre, NSW 2153, Australia

Sterling ISBN 0-8069-0987-0

CONTENTS

They call us
The Alligators.

That's because Alligators don't quit, and neither do we. Once an Alligator gets you in its jaws, you don't have a chance. And once we get on the track of a criminal—he or she doesn't have a chance either. We're all good at detective work, and we never give up. We're also a pretty snappy bunch, too. There are four of us:

Liza

Carlos

Poppy

Alex

The Alligators

Name: Alex
Nickname: Shrunken
Head, Gnome, Dwarf
Age: 13
Zodiac Sign: Capricorn
Hobbies: Change weekly,
but usually involve sports
Favorite Food:
Everything
Distinguishing Marks:
I'm the shortest kid in my
class and used to get teased because of that. Today
nobody dares to tease me anymore because I've gotten
to be the best athlete in school.

Name: Liza
Nickname: Superbrain
Age: 13
Zodiac Sign: Cancer
Hobbies: Skiing and
hiking
Favorite Food: Chinese food
(I use chopsticks)
Distinguishing Marks:
Have two long blond braids
that I'm very proud of. I
devour every crime thriller
that I can get hold of and
learn techniques from the pros.

Name: Paula
Nickname: Poppy
Age: 9
Zodiac Sign: Pisces
Hobbies: My animals
Favorite Food: Fruit salad
(no meat)
Distinguishing Marks: I
own two dogs, a parrot,
three cats, rabbits, goldfish,
rats, and a hamster. Stray
animals often come to visit.

Name: Carlos
Nickname: Hamlet's Father
Age: 10
Zodiac Sign: Libra
Hobbies: Reading. I remember almost everything once
I've read it.
Favorite Food: Spaghetti
Distinguishing Marks: My parents are actors and I
have already appeared on stage and in film, too.
Sometimes I talk kind of obscurely, which makes
others mad.

HI, DETECTIVE AND ALLIGATORS BUDDY!

Here it is—our secret book. In it, we have written down many of the tips and techniques that we have collected in the course of our detective work.

- Tips for detective equipment
- Tips for what to do at a crime scene and during investigations
- Alligator techniques that we invented for our cases
- Tips for really secret signs, secret writing, secret languages, and secret messages
- Tips for reading tracks
- Tips for outdoor adventures
- Ideas for your detective and Alligator training

At the end of this book, you'll find a major Alligator Detective test.

Have fun studying this secret book. You'll discover fantastic things here. Try them out. Only techniques you've really mastered can be useful later on.

Important: The tasks and questions in the test are all connected to the tips and techniques in the book. Read it very carefully. Take your time when you start the test. It's best to solve the problems one after the other.

Stay on track! And remember—

never quit!

DETECTIVE EQUIPMENT

Observation Newspaper

Alligators Detective Room

Umbrella with a Rear View

Shoebox Camera

CLICK

ALLIGATORS NOTEBOOK

This is what you need:

- A notebook for jotting down your observations. You can also use it for secret messages and to measure articles you find or tracks. It's a good idea to pick one with heavy cardboard covers. A spiral binding works best.

It is also important to note how big an article is. Your notebook can double as a ruler.

This is how you prepare it:

Using a ruler, mark inches on the long side of the inside front cover of your notebook.

On the same page we jotted down the secret signs of our Alligators team. This makes it easy to write a secret message quickly, or to decode one.

This is how it works:

When we open the notebook, we see the secret signs and can write a message immediately. It also works the other way: We put a message that we have received inside the notebook and decode the signs.

DETECTIVE TRAINING

Grab your notebook and off you go. Look for a "crime scene." It could be a clearing in the forest, for example, a parking lot, a certain house or classroom. Record everything that catches your eye.

SECRET NOTES

You might get caught and searched for secret writing. But all your enemies could find would be an old math notebook—nothing else! Actually, the book contains many top secret messages.

This is what you need:
- An old math notebook
- A pen with "invisible" ink

This is how you do it:
The technique is very easy, but also very good. You write your secret messages with "invisible ink" between the lines in your notebook. This hides the notes extremely well. If you want to read them, warm the book over a radiator or a hot light bulb—carefully, of course!

- Never push so hard that the secret message doesn't stay secret.
- Never dry the ink with blotting paper.
- Always give the letters time to dry—at least an hour.

You can also hide a message between the lines of a perfectly harmless letter.

Read about invisible ink on page 55.

PEOPLE FILES

In these files you can keep all the information about people that you know or those you observe. These files can be very useful.

This is what you need:
- Index cards

This is how you do it:
Mark the cards like this:

Name:

Age:

Address:

Telephone
   number:

e-mail address:

Height:

Weight:

Distinguishing
   marks:

Birthday:

Zodiac sign:

Likes a lot:

Dislikes:

Notes:

DETECTIVE TRAINING
Compose a "people file" about someone you do not know personally but only observe.

THE ALLIGATORS
DETECTIVE SUITCASE

This suitcase contains everything you need when you want to search for tracks. The smaller it is, the better.

This is what you need:

- A notebook
- A pen and pencil
- Fingerprint powder
- Magnifying glass
- Tweezers
- Tape measure
- Flashlight
- Envelopes (for keeping suspicious articles)
- Large pieces of paper that you can use to copy foot-prints, for example
- A camera
- A small pocketknife or small scissors
- Colorful crayons or markers for secret signs
- A whistle for emergencies and to communicate across great distances
- Coins (for phone calls) or a phone card
- Rubber gloves, so that you don't destroy clues at a crime scene or leave your fingerprints

This is how you do it:

Take an old beauty case, a sewing kit, or a small overnight bag and cover it with paper or fabric. Divide the inside of the case by inserting cardboard or little boxes. It is important to keep this neat so that you can find everything quickly.

THE MINI-DETECTIVE SUITCASE

It's no bigger than a matchbox—in fact, it is a matchbox! It looks inconspicuous, but it still contains many useful things for detectives. You can write secret messages using the mini-suitcase, take fingerprints, make notes, leave secret signs, and much more. When strangers open the suitcase, they will think it's just a matchbox. Only members of your group will know that they have to pull up the cover and find the equipment underneath.

This is what you need:
- A matchbox
- Tiny pencils
- Tape
- Thin string
- A small piece of crayon
- A small container or tube with a stopper in it
- Thin cardboard
- A piece of wax
- Paper
- Talcum powder or pencil dust
- A small brush
- Colorful clips

This is how you do it:
- Cut the cardboard as shown in the drawing.
- Glue some old, used matchsticks to the cardboard. They will serve as your cover. Attach a piece of string to the edge, so that you can open the cover easily.
- Glue the cardboard into the box.
- Tie the tape for fingerprints around one of the pencils.
- Cut thin paper in small pieces and attach them, making a mini notepad.

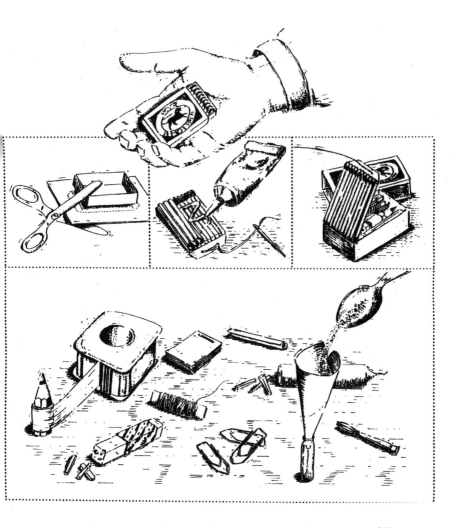

- Make a small funnel from paper and use it to fill a little tube with powder or pencil dust.
- To get a small paper roll with just enough room for a message, wrap tracing paper around some of the used matches.
- Cut small pieces from the crayons and a wax candle (more about wax on page 56).
- Wrap the string around a piece of cardboard.

SECRET CAMERAS

It is possible to photograph people without their knowledge! You just have to have your camera well hidden. Here are a few tips on how to turn your ordinary camera into a secret camera.

This is what you need:
- A backpack or an old bag
- A shoebox
- A scissors

BACKPACK CAMERA:
Cut a hole in the backpack large enough to fit around the camera lens. Put the camera into the backpack so that the lens looks right through the hole. Then you have to be able to push the shutter release. This takes some practice. It is important to hold the backpack in a way that does not look suspicious.

THE SHOEBOX CAMERA
Cut a small hole in the shoebox. Be careful to hide the hole in the price tag or the company name. Tape the camera so that it is exactly in front of the hole on the inside of the shoebox. Cut a large hole in the back of the box so you can stick your hand inside. When you are ready to take a picture, push the shutter release.

If your camera does not forward the film automatically, you'll need to do that manually also.

DETECTIVE TIP

Practice in front of a mirror holding the box without causing suspicion.

ALLIGATORS TIP

Since you can't focus through a viewfinder, you need to practice taking pictures with your secret camera. Soon you'll get a feeling for the distance you need between you and another person in order to get them completely in the picture.

Figure out what appears in the photograph when you hold the camera at stomach height. Put the camera on a table and look through the viewfinder. Your buddy can play the suspect and pose in front of the camera. Are head and legs in the picture? Then the distance is right!

UMBRELLA WITH A REAR VIEW

Was Scarface still following Alex, Liza, Poppy, and Carlos? The Alligators did not want to let the suspect know that they were aware of his presence. Turning around was out of the question. But they did not need to do that. They had an umbrella with a rear view.

This is what you need:
- An umbrella
- A small mirror
- Rubber bands

This is how you do it:

Open the umbrella and attach the mirror with the rubber bands.

ALLIGATORS FLASHLIGHT

It is very easy to send signals with this flashlight.

This is what you need:
- A flashlight (torch) with a smooth handle
- See-through tape
- The blink code

This is how you do it:
Copy the code shown below onto the handle of the flashlight. Then wrap a large piece of the see-through, self-adhesive tape over the code around the handle and attach it well by rubbing. Done!

The most important blink signs:
- Help!—Fast left and right movements with the flashlight
- Come here!—A circle
- Are you okay?—Three blinks
- Good!—One blink
- Bad!—Two blinks
- This is boring—Wavy lines
- I have a surprise for you—Zigzag lines
- Do not come here!—Quick up and down
- Good night!—Five blinks

ALLIGATORS TIP
Invent your own signs.

OBSERVATION NEWSPAPER AND OBSERVATION BOOK

This is an old technique, but it still works.

This is what you need:
- A newspaper
- An old book

This is how you do it:
Rip a small hole in the crease of the newspaper. You can now pretend to read, but in actuality you are observing the suspect through the hole.

The observation book is even better. You make a hole in the back of an old book. The hole shouldn't be too small, but make sure to hide it in the writing or in a picture on the back cover of the book. Open the book and you can peep through the observation hole.

CASE BOX

Everyone thinks the box contains a game, cornflakes, or detergent. In reality, it holds secret messages, photos, or pieces of evidence you have found.

This is what you need:
- Empty boxes from games, candy, detergent, or similar things.

Inside the boxes you can hide your notes, pieces of evidence, and photos for the case you're working on.

ALLIGATORS DETECTIVE ROOM

This is how you can transform your room into a more secure facility.

THE DOOR

- Hang a small bell on a long nail over the door. This way, no one can enter your room without your hearing it.
- Make inconspicuous marks on the doorframe. Then, if someone comes in, you will know immediately how tall he or she is.
- When you leave the room, always paste a thread between the door and the doorframe. If, when you get back, the thread has fallen down, somebody has paid you a visit.
- You can do the same thing with a few strands of hair.
- The next trick works only with doors that open outwards: When you leave the room, put a crumpled piece of paper in front of the door. It should look as if someone dropped it by accident. The paper should not be too big or conspicuous. If you come back and see that the paper has moved, you will know that someone has opened the door.

THE DESK

- While you are sitting down, you always need to be able to see the door. A simple mirror can help you with that.

- Hide a tape recorder on the desk, which you can use to record conversations.

THE WINDOW
- Always have binoculars handy.

WASTEBASKET
- Install a false bottom. You can hide things underneath it.

SHELF
- Fake a secret hiding place, in which you keep nothing important. It is there to be found and distract attention from your real hiding place. The real hiding place for your money, evidence, and other things is elsewhere.

THE WALL
- Draw a map of your neighborhood.
- A bulletin board will serve as a hiding place for photos, notes, messages, and other things.

SECRET CAMERA
- Always have your secret camera ready to take pictures. Keep handkerchiefs in the box that you keep your camera in. That way you can take one out after pushing the shutter release—a great way to distract people's attention.

ALARM LAMP
- Underneath your desk, keep a foot switch for a special lamp. Cut the word "ALARM" into an old lampshade and cover the letters with tracing paper. Without the light on, no one will be able to see the word. But when you step on the switch, people will see it clearly.

ALLIGATORS TIP

When you travel during vacations or holidays, take an empty wallet with you. You can use the holidays to collect things for your wallet so that you can make people believe you're someone else. Also get yourself a small calendar from a shop at the holiday resort.

Coins, a few bills, a bus ticket, stamps, and a few things that obviously came from that special place should be enough. Get your picture taken in front of a well-known landmark that tells people where you are.

Write names, addresses, and invented dates in your calendar that also connect you to that special place. You can get the names from street signs, telephone books, shops, and so on. Use places for your dates that you have actually visited.

DID SOMEONE READ YOUR LETTER?

- If your letter is lying on a pile of papers, draw a
pencil line across the side
border of the pile before
you leave the room. If,
when you return, the line
is broken, someone has
messed with your papers.
- To find out whether
someone has read a folded
letter, sprinkle a few hair
strands, powder, or confetti
in the folded letter. These
things will fall out if the letter
gets opened and is read. If they
are gone when you return, you
will know that someone has been
snooping around your things.

HAS SOMEONE BEEN GOING THROUGH YOUR CLOSET OR CABINET?

- Push a small piece of wire or a paper
clip between the closet or cabinet door
and the door frame. It will fall out if
someone opens the door.
- Attach a piece of tape
underneath the drawer of
the cabinet in the space
between drawers. If some-
one opens the drawer, it
will fall off.

ALL-NATURAL ALARM SYSTEMS

You can build good alarm systems with simple things.
- Hang two or three wire hangers on the inside of your door or window. When the door or window is opened, the hangers will clink.
- Slightly crumpled papers or foil on the floor behind you will tell you immediately when someone is trying to sneak up on you.
- An inflated balloon in a desk drawer can create a loud bang. Attach a pin or needle to it, so that the balloon bursts when the drawer is opened.

TIN-CAN ALARM SYSTEMS
Empty cans make great alarm systems, too.
- Tie a can to a string and hang it on the doorknob. If someone opens the door, the can will alert you.
- Even better: Tie two sticks at one end and lean them like an upside-down V against the door. At the crossing point of the two sticks, attach a can on a string. When the door is opened, the sticks and the can collapse and warn you.

HOW FAR AWAY IS THE SUSPECT?

You can guess the distance between you and a suspect with one glance.

165 feet (50m): You recognize the face and see eyes and mouth.

330 feet (100m): The eyes register only as black dots.

660 feet (200m): The face is still visible. You can still see buttons, pockets, and belts.

990 feet (300m): The face seems to be one undivided area. You cannot recognize eyes and mouth any longer.

1650 feet (500m): You can see only the outline of a person, but you can still tell whether the suspect is wearing a hat and what color his or her clothes are.

1980 feet (600m): The head seems to be only a light dot.

2310 feet (700m): Head and body melt together into one large dot.

ALLIGATORS TRAINING

Try this out with your friends. Go to a large field or avenue. Determine the distances and get into position. Then one of you runs off a little bit. The others turn around and guess how far away their buddy is.

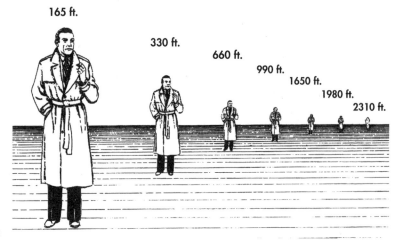

165 ft.   330 ft.   660 ft.   990 ft.   1650 ft.   1980 ft.   2310 ft.

HOW DO YOU LOSE A PURSUER?

You can feel it—you know it—someone is following you! Someone is sticking to your heels and always keeping a bit behind. How can you lose this "shadow"?

This is how you do it:

- The easiest way: Dive into a cluster of people. If there are many people around you, mingle and hide. Your pursuer may lose you.
- Pro technique: Take a very conspicuous cap or a thin raincoat with you when you go out. This way you can change your appearance in a flash. Your pursuer will still be looking for your original outfit.
- Reversible jackets are great, too. The jacket is red on the outside and blue on the inside, for example. You only have to turn it inside out and you're wearing a different color.
- Run into a building and leave through the back door.
- If you have no other choice, hide in a pitch-dark place, turn on your flashlight, and position it so that it looks as if you're holding it in your hand. Then leave it and quickly get out of there. Your pursuer will think that you are still sitting in your hiding place, because he or she will only be looking at the light.

HOW DO YOU CAMOUFLAGE YOURSELF?

Camouflaging means changing your appearance so that you are not recognized. That way you can investigate more easily and quietly.

THE BEST TRICKS
Change your face:

- Hair gel makes it very simple to change your hairstyle. Rub the gel into your hair and comb it back.
- You don't wear glasses? Put some on.
- A missing tooth really changes your face. Of course, you don't have to knock a tooth out. Actors use tooth black. This tints the tooth black, and from a distance it looks like a hole. Check it out. You'll be amazed how much this can do.
- At the dentist's office, you sometimes get little cotton rolls put in your mouth. These can help you get hamster cheeks. Ask your dentist for a few rolls during your next visit and try it out. (It might make your visit to the dentist fun for once.)
- Protruding ears can change your appearance. If you are using glasses to help camouflage yourself, wrap a thick layer of wet plaster around the ear-pieces. That will make your ears stick out.
- Thicken your eyebrows using an eyebrow pencil.

CAMOUFLAGE IN A FLASH

Suddenly you look more beefy from behind!

This is what you need:
- A hat
- A towel

Both can be carried in a bag during your investigations.

This is how you do it:
- Roll up the towel lengthwise and put it on your shoulders. Put on a coat on top of the towel. You will look as if you have high, broad shoulders. Pull up the collar and put on the hat. You'll look like a different person from behind.

THE GIANT MIRROR

There are many giant mirrors on the street in which you can observe what is happening behind you. The great thing is that your pursuers will not even know that you're doing it.

This is how you do it:

Stand in front of a shop window. You can observe what happens behind you in the plate glass.

Note: Don't get too close to the window or the giant mirror will not work.

HOW YOU CAN LOOK THROUGH FROSTED GLASS

You know what frosted glass is like. It's white and opaque. But with this simple technique, you can look through it, nonetheless.

This is what you need:

• See-through tape

This is how you do it:

Attach a piece of tape to the frosted glass and rub it on tight with your thumb. The frosted glass becomes transparent!

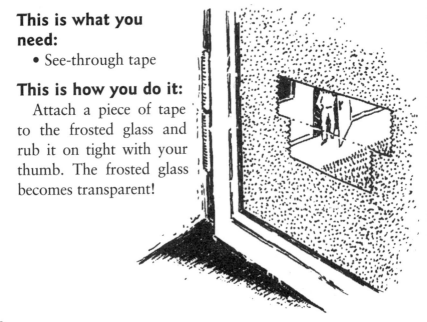

THE PENCIL TRICK

The telephone rang. Percy K. picked up the receiver and said quietly, "Hello."

"We have exposed your technique," a strangely nasal voice informed him. "Quit your stealing and return all the stolen goods and we won't tell on you."

Then only the dial tone was audible.

Percy K. hung up and wiped his forehead. He had dropped the stolen goods into the closed umbrella of a stranger at the shop. The innocent stranger had smuggled the loot outside the store without realizing he had it.

The Alligators had observed Percy K. but did not turn him over to the police since he was their schoolmate.

Whose strange voice was this? Who called Percy K.?

This is how you do it:

The voice was Poppy's. She kept a pencil between her teeth while she talked. This technique completely transformed her voice. But before you try it, practice talking with the pencil in your teeth. Make sure that you'll be understood but not exposed!

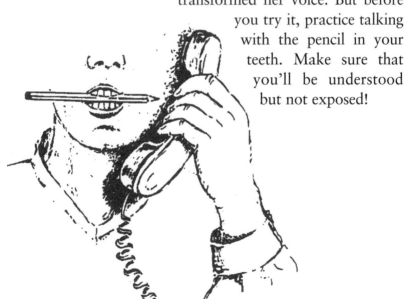

THE RASPING VOICE

Do you know what a kazoo is? You can get it in toy stores. When you put it in your mouth and sing into it, your voice sounds like a trumpet. It completely distorts your voice. Talk into it and you sound like a cross between Donald Duck and Frankenstein!

THE GLASS ON THE WALL

Alex was caught. The mysterious Signore Brazi had discovered him and locked him up. Now Brazi was in the next room talking on the phone. But Alex couldn't understand what he was saying.

Then, with a little trick, Alex listened in on the conversation. He learned that Signore Brazi wanted to take his captive away that evening. Alex did not have much time to escape.

How did Alex manage to hear the conversation?

This is how you do it:

Alex found a regular drinking glass, put the open end against the wall, and pressed his ear against the bottom of the glass.

Note: This works best with a tall glass with thin sides.

33

FALSE LEADS

A great trick! Your pursuers are looking at the ground. There they find your shoeprints. They follow the tracks and suddenly stand at the edge of a cliff.
Did you jump into the depths?

This is how you do it:

Of course, you didn't jump. You simply walked backwards away from the cliff. But your tracks make it look as if you had run towards the edge!

LIP READING

Carlos is a master of lip reading. He can SEE what someone is saying through a closed window.

Lip reading is not that difficult. You just have to practice distinguishing the letters from each other. The "M," "A," and "U" will not be a problem for you.

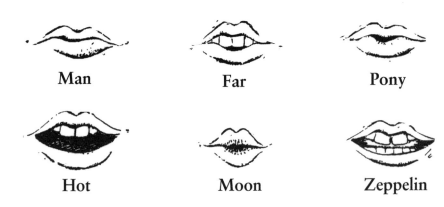

Man	Far	Pony
Hot	Moon	Zeppelin

A PLAN DISAPPEARS

Whenever an Alligator uses a plan or drawing, it is attached to a long piece of elastic. If someone comes along who should not see it, the paper quickly disappears into the Alligator's jacket—with no noticeable movement!

This is what you need:
- An elastic band—the kind sewn at the top of your pants (you can find it in a sewing shop)
- A safety pin
- A piece of cardboard about 1″ × 1½ ″ (4 × 6cm) in size
- 4 paper clips

This is how you do it:
- Make a large hole in the cardboard and staple or sew the band to it. Attach the safety pin to the other end. Attach the pin at the shoulder inside your jacket.
- The cardboard should be at the lower end of your arm. If you want to take it out, slip your other hand inside your sleeve, grab it and pull it out.
- Then hold the cardboard at the end attached to the band. Attach your plan to the cardboard with four paper clips.
- If you want to make the plan disappear, simply let go of the cardboard. It slides back into your sleeve

THE BANDAGE TRICK

You can hide small articles and messages behind a bandage. Alex has a slightly gross trick: He draws brown spots on the bandage with a pen, so that it looks old and bloodied.

HIDING PLACE IN A SHOELACE

Once Carlos was caught by crooks when he was carrying an important and secret message. But although they thoroughly searched him, they couldn't find anything. They even checked his mouth for the message. So where was it?

It was in the mini-pocket on his shoelace.

This is what you need:
- Shoes with shoelaces
- A piece of cloth
- Needle
- String
- Tweezers

This is how you do it:

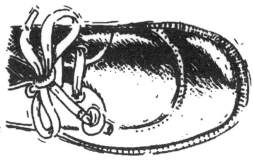

- Sew a tiny capsule from the cloth.
- Attach it to the end of the lace. It will look like a knot.
- Wrap your secret message around a pencil to get it small enough to stuff into the mini-pocket.
- Using tweezers, you can get it out again.

SECRET SIGNS AND SECRET LANGUAGES

TRAMP MARKINGS

What are these markings? They're secret signs that tramps used to use to tell other tramps what was going on in the area. They "marked" houses where they could get rich pickings—let others know whether generous people or skinflints lived in a house, and so on. The markings were either written on house walls with chalk or drawn on the ground with a stone.

TRAMP MARKINGS

╫	Attention—Danger!
⊘	You can get food here.
✕	You won't get anything here.
⌣	You can sleep here.
OᴏO	You can get money here.
‖∩∩✗	Three kids, two women, and a man live here.
✕ ✗ ✗ → °	You'll get something on the third floor to your right.
◁══◗	You'll get something here, but you'll have to work for it.

CROOK MARKINGS

The markings that criminals use may differ from place to place. Here are a few marks that were often visible. Keep your eyes open. Maybe you'll find one of these messages from earlier days—on the walls of an old house.

You won't get anything here.

Get out right away!

The owners call the cops.

This house is dangerous.

A cop lives here.

Money to steal here.

Here all you can get is food.

Careful—dog bites!

Pretend to be sick—
that works here.

Come at night.

Come in the morning.

Don't steal anything here.

You'll get beat up here!

HAND SIGNS

Using hand signs, you can tell others something without saying a word. It is important that the signs not be too obvious.

Quiet!

Listen!

Look there!

Yes.

No.

All.

Fear (index finger shakes)

Fire!

Good!

ALLIGATOR TRAINING

Invent more signs. You are probably already using some with your friends. What do your signs look like for these messages, for example?

- Are we going home?
- Bigger!
- To the left
- I'm hungry!

- I want ice cream.
- Smaller!
- To the right
- Careful . . .

THE FINGER ALPHABET WITH ONE HAND

Maybe you already know the finger alphabet. You can use these signs to pass messages at school. They have been proven to work many times.

A

B   **C**   **D**   **E**   **F**

G   **H**   **I**   **J**   **K**

L   **M**   **N**   **O**   **P**

Q   **R**   **S**   **T**   **U**

V   **W**   **X**   **Y**   **Z**   41

THE FINGER ALPHABET WITH TWO HANDS

A–R

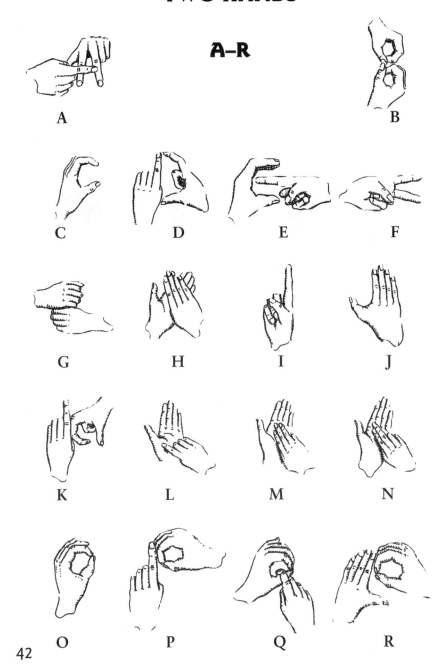

A

B

C

D

E

F

G

H

I

J

K

L

M

N

O

P

Q

R

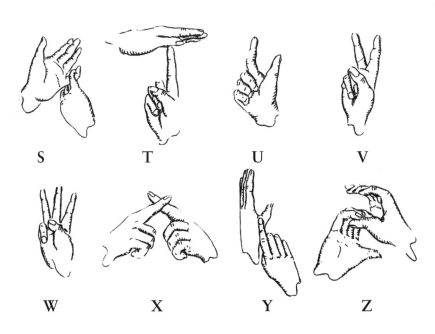

S T U V

W X Y Z

THE MORSE ALPHABET

You can tap or blink Morse code. And while you're doing it, it looks like you're just dreaming, tapping on the table with your pencil.

THE FINGER LANGUAGE OF DIVERS

You may have to dive underwater sometime. We have had to. During a diving course, we not only learned how to handle oxygen, glasses, and flippers, but we also learned the language of divers. The signs are easy to remember. We sometimes use them on land, too.

 Everything is all right—okay!

 Something is not right. I have a bad feeling.

 I'm coming out. or Come out!

 I'm diving down. or Come, dive down!

 I've opened my reserve tank.

 I don't have any more air!

 Open my reserve tank.

 Emergency! Help!

 I

 You

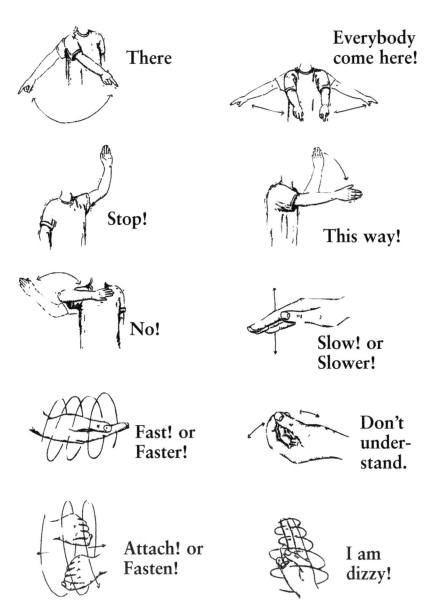

There

Everybody come here!

Stop!

This way!

No!

Slow! or Slower!

Fast! or Faster!

Don't under-stand.

Attach! or Fasten!

I am dizzy!

Use a flashlight to signal underwater if you dive at night.
- Circling the flashlight: Everything is fine.
- Moving the flashlight up and down: Something is wrong!

THE FLAG ALPHABET

With two flags, you can transmit letters, words, and whole sentences. Flag language is useful for passing on messages from a distance—from a mountaintop to a valley, for example.

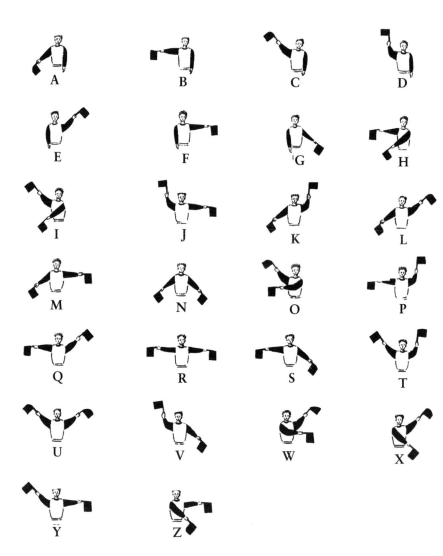

SECRET AGENT SIGNS

1 One hand in pocket = Yes. **2** Two hands in pockets = No.
3 Scratching head = Careful, danger! **4** Scratching neck = Careful, enemies. **5** Crossed legs = Meet in hiding place. **6** Hands in back = We're not together. **7** Scratching ear = We'll talk later on phone. **8** Scratching eye = Have something to show you. **9** Cross one leg = Leaving soon. **10** Scratching nose = Careful, they know who you are. **11** Crossed arms = Have message for you. **12** Combing hair = I won't stay long. **13** Pushing glasses upwards twice = See you tomorrow. **14** Tapping lips = Come with me. **15** Pulling earlobe = You'd better leave.

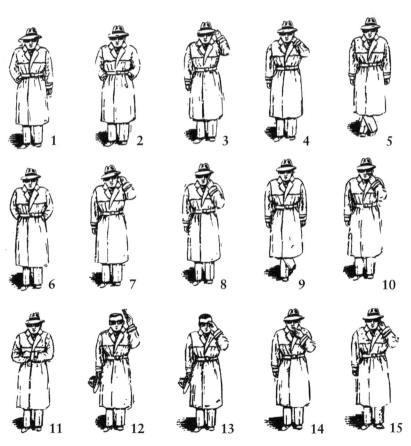

THE PILOT ALPHABET

When people need to be very careful spelling a word, they not only say single letters: There could be misunderstandings, especially with "E," "G," "D," and such sounds. So they use a word for each letter. In aviation, the same words are used for spelling all over the world. Here they are:

A—ALFA	N—NOVEMBER
B—BRAVO	O—OSCAR
C—CHARLIE	P—PAPA
D—DELTA	Q—QUEBEC
E—ECHO	R—ROMEO
F—FOXTROT	S—SIERRA
G—GOLF	T—TANGO
H—HOTEL	U—UNIFORM
I—INDIA	V—VICTOR
J—JULIET	W—WHISKEY
K—KILO	X—X-RAY
L—LIMA	Y—YANKEE
M—MIKE	Z—ZULU

For example, ALLIGATORS is spelled like this:

ALFA LIMA LIMA INDIA GOLF ALFA TANGO OSCAR ROMEO SIERRA

EMERGENCY LANGUAGE
FOR PILOTS

Liza's family once crashed a small plane in the rainforest. Later a pilot told them that there were emergency signs you can use in cases like this. These signs are made with stones and should be large enough to be seen from the air by search planes.

Here are the most important signs:

I — We need a doctor!

F — We need food!

△ — Landing is impossible!

U — Our plane is kaput!

X — Do not land!

Y — Yes!

LL — Everything is okay.

N — No!

☐ — Drop a map and compass.
We'll find our way.

↑ — We walked here.

TV CODE SENTENCES

"Today they are showing a cool film on TV at 6:30."

Information? Yes, but not what you think. It means: "Today we'll meet at 6:30 p.m." If you add, "It's on Channel 4," this means: "Meet in the basement." If you say, "It's on Channel 2," this means: "In the attic."

You can make up codes for all the places and things you want to do.

Example: "I've got the dentist at 3:00."

Means: "Meet at the tree house."

Of course, all your friends must know the code.

SECRET SIGNS FOR HANDSHAKES

Super cool! Imagine that you are supposed to meet a special agent, but you don't know him or her, and have no clue as to what they might look like. You only know that a party was chosen as a meeting place.

Ten people are introduced to you at the party. But who is your contact person? You know immediately, because he or she shakes your hand in a very special way.

Examples:

- You bend your thumb inward while shaking hands. If the other person does this as well, you know whom you're dealing with. Everyone else will simply think you're a little strange.
- While shaking hands, you pat the person three times on the arm with your left hand. If he or she pats you back, that's your colleague.
- You form a fist twice after shaking hands and watch to see whether the person does the same thing.

SECRET WRITING

RULER MESSAGE

What would you think if you received a ruler as a message? Probably, "Huh? What's that supposed to mean?" But ruler messages can be useful, and encoding messages is very quick.

This is what you need:
- A ruler
- A pencil
- Paper

This is how it works:

Put the ruler on a piece of paper and clearly mark Zero with a line. At 1 you start your message. At each inch mark, you add another letter of your message.

To make the message unreadable by those who aren't in on the code, fill in any letters you want in the empty spaces.

When your buddies receive this message, they simply have to put down the ruler and make sure that Zero is at the first line. Then they read the letters at the inch marks and can quickly decode the message.

MESSAGE WITH STARS

How many people would get suspicious about a piece of paper with a few stars on it? Surely no one. But it actually could contain an important message.

This is what you need:
- Graph paper
- A pencil
- Cardboard
- Glue

Attach a row of 26 squares to a piece of cardboard. Write a letter in each box. This will make encoding and decoding easier. Keep this cardboard for future use.

This is how it works:
Put the cardboard with the letters on the paper so that A is at the out-ermost left-hand box. Make a star in the first row above the first letter of your message. Now move down the line and make a

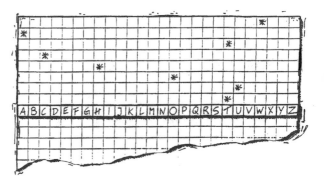

star above the second letter of your message. The decoding works the same way. Put down the letter row and move down line by line.

ALLIGATORS TIP
We always note down the letters at the edge of the paper. But be careful to tear up the decoded message immediately after reading it.

MYSTERIOUS NUMBERS

A great code! So far, few people have managed to break it! Unfortunately, it takes a long time to encode a message this way. This is how one of them looks:

145723 2157543 143 57214

It means "Help."

This is what you need:
- The model shown here

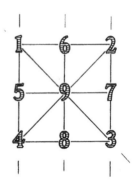

This is how it works:
The numbers show how the specific letter is written. Connect the numbers and they make up the letter. We always give the numbers so that they can be written with one single line. K, for example, would be 6929398.

54

INVISIBLE INK—THE BEST SECRET INKS

The technique is simple. You write with ink that disappears once it dries. Only members of your team can make it visible.

I. LEMON INK

Squeeze the lemon and run the juice through a coffee filter. In order to make lemon juice visible, the message has to be heated above a radiator or a light bulb.

2. ONION JUICE

It is not easy to produce this ink. In addition, you may begin to cry. That's how onions are. The best way to process the onion is to mash it against a grater and then put it into a tea sieve. Use a spoon to press out the juice. When the onion ink is heated, it turns black.

3. VINEGAR

White vinegar is best. It turns reddish when heated.

4. MILK

It is easiest to apply milk with a brush. Leave the milk letter out to dry for a long time. This writing also becomes visible by heating it.

WHAT IS THE BEST WAY TO WRITE WITH THESE INKS?

We use old fountain pens, which we clean thoroughly. You can also use a clean brush, a quill pen, or a toothpick.

WAX MESSAGES

This is what you need:
- A pencil-shaped piece of candle wax
- Paper
- Cocoa or pencil dust

This is how you do it:
Write a message with the wax pencil on white paper. When your buddies are ready to make the message visible, they sprinkle a bit of cocoa or pencil dust on it and rub it softly over the page. Soon they can see the letters.

WATER WRITING

You can also write secret letters without ink.

This is what you need:
- 2 pages of typewriter paper
- A mirror
- Water
- Pen or pencil

This is how it works:
- First, dip one piece of paper in water. Then put it on a smooth surface. A glass plate or mirror is best for this. Smooth out the paper.
- Put a dry piece of paper on top of it. Write your message with pencil or pen on this page.
- Peel off the dry sheet and destroy it.
- When the wet page is dry, it's ready. The paper looks completely innocent.
- Those who want to read the letter simply have to dip it in water and the writing becomes visible.

ALLIGATORS TIP
Write a pointless message on the top half of the page and use the bottom half for the water writing.

BOOK MESSAGES

Books are excellent for secret messages.

This is what you need:

- 2 identical books. They should not only have the same title, but should be from the same edition. You have one book, your buddy has the other one.
- Paper
- A pencil or pen

This is how it works:

- **Technique 1:** Your friend gets a note with the following message:

    22.19 67.45 98.26 7.9 56.33

    This means: Go to page 22, take the 19th word.
    Go to page 67, look for the 45th word.
    On to page 98, look for the 26th word.
    On page 7, take the 9th word.
    On page 56, take the 33rd.

Put these words together and get the message.

- **Technique 2:** Put a thin white page onto a book page. Mark the first and last letter of the page with a dot. Then draw a circle around each letter that you need for the message—one after the other. Don't forget to agree with your buddies ahead of time about which page you'll be using.

Your buddies now simply have to put the paper in the same spot in their book. The black dots show the positions of the first and last letter. Now your buddies can connect the circled letters in order to get the message.

THE IMPOSSIBLE-TO-FIND MESSAGE

Send a usual letter. Write the actual secret message with a hard pencil in tiny letters (encoded for safety reasons) on the envelope, where the stamp gets attached. Put on the stamp and send it.

Your buddies simply have to cut out the upper edge and put it in a bowl of hot water. The stamp will loosen and the message appear.

HOW DO YOU DECODE OTHER PEOPLE'S SECRET MESSAGES?

The most important techniques:

- If you find a secret message, check it out carefully. The signs can stand either for letters or for whole words.
- Identical signs mean identical letters. In every text there are many "E's." "S's," "H's," and "T's" are also common.
- Replace them one after another with the most common letters. That may give you a lead.
- Can you detect spaces between certain signs? The signs between spaces may make up a word.
- Try to decipher very short words first. Often that will pave the way to the longer words.
- When you recognize a letter, immediately insert it into the rest of the text.

Cracking a code takes time—a lot of patience and time. Today computers are used for decoding. But even they cannot always crack a good code right away.

CLUES AND TRACKS

GATHERING CLUES

Clues can be:
- Cloth fibers or threads
- A paper with writing
- Tooth marks in chocolate
- A chewing-gum loop
- A ticket
- A button
- Cigarette butts
- Lipstick on a glass
- A lost pen
- A footprint
- Fingerprints
- Hairs
- Tire tracks
- Splinters
- A lighter

This is how you gather clues:

1. Carefully examine everything you find with a magnifying glass and test it. Use tweezers to put the found article in a little plastic bag or in a paper envelope.

2. Label every piece with:
> Where found
> When found
> Suspicion

FINGERPRINTS

There aren't two people in the whole world with the same fingerprints. Therefore, fingerprints are among the best evidence to use to catch a criminal.

This is what you need:

1. A soft brush
2. Fingerprint powder
3. Adhesive tape
4. Small white or black cards

FINGERPRINT POWDER

There are three kinds:

1. You can use very fine body powder.
2. You can buy charcoal in an art store and grate it into a fine powder with sandpaper.
3. You can use sandpaper to grate a pencil lead into fine powder.

This is how you do it:

- Empty the powder into a small bag or box.
- Using the brush, dot the powder onto the area in question until the fingerprint becomes visible. Blow off the rest of the unnecessary powder.
- Press see-through tape—sticky side down—onto the spot that you have covered with powder. Attach it thoroughly, with your fingernails, if possible.
- When you pull off the tape, the fingerprint will be on it.
- Attach the tape to a card. (If you have taken the fingerprint with white powder, put it on a black card.) Put others on a white card.
- Label the card as follows:
  Person: Time:
  Date: Place:

Naturally, you can fingerprint all your friends and start a real database. A water-soluble stamp pad is best for that. Push their fingers into the stamp pad, then press their fingertips onto a piece of paper.

HOW DO YOU FIND FINGERPRINTS?

The most important tips:
- Do not touch anything or you will leave finger-prints as well! Open doors with your elbows.
- Wearing gloves is good. But be careful, you can still destroy the culprit's fingerprints.
- Search the crime scene in circles that increase in size. Examine all articles and pieces of furniture.
- Ask yourself what the culprit might have touched. Examine the articles in question.
- Take notes as to where else you want to use finger-print powder as soon as you finish your search.

Places where fingerprints can be found:
- Windows (Did the culprit come in through the window? Did he touch the glass?)
- Varnished furniture, plates, picture frames
- Vases, bottles, and glasses
- Valuable papers

This is how to examine things without touching them:
- Always use tweezers to pick up small things.
- If you want to examine the out-side of a glass, slip your fingers inside it, spread them, and you'll be able to lift the glass easily.
- Open drawers by using a pencil.
- Slide windows open and closed with a ruler.

ANALYZING FINGERPRINTS

Here are some examples of what fingerprints can look like. We will point out the most important features that human fingers have. Of course, they all differ in size and never are identical.

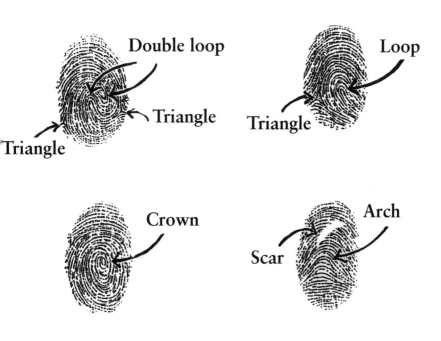

To be able to say that a suspect's fingerprint is the same as a print found at the crime scene, you should find at least two corresponding traits. There is a real danger of accusing an innocent person!

FOOTPRINTS

We have observed and recorded various footprints:

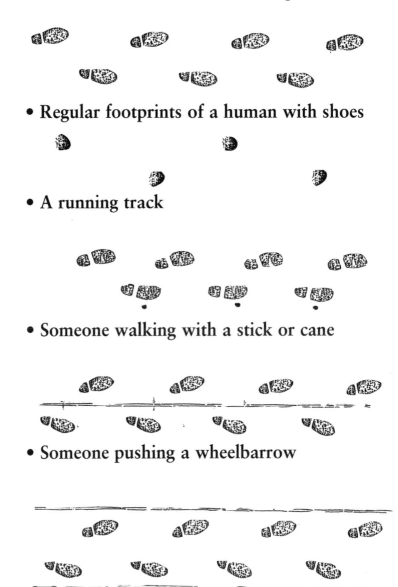

- **Regular footprints of a human with shoes**

- **A running track**

- Someone walking with a stick or cane

- Someone pushing a wheelbarrow

- Someone pulling a cart

- Steps made by a large person

- A man and a woman walking next to each other

- A person with a dog

- Someone on crutches

- Someone carrying something heavy and leaving deep imprints

WHICH TRACK COMES FROM WHICH SHOE?

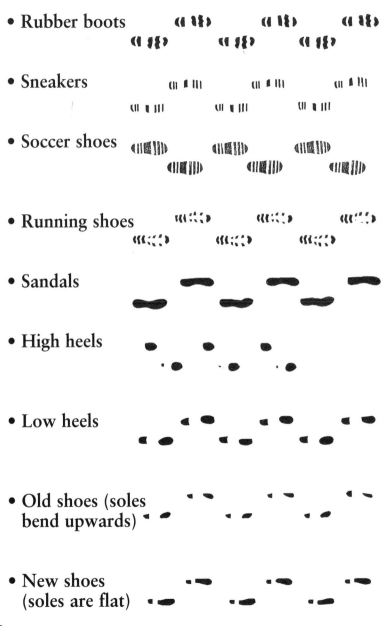

- Rubber boots
- Sneakers
- Soccer shoes
- Running shoes
- Sandals
- High heels
- Low heels
- Old shoes (soles bend upwards)
- New shoes (soles are flat)

ANIMAL TRACKS

- Cat

- Dog

- Sheep

- Deer

- Bear

  hind paw   front paw

- Wolf

- Fox

- Rabbit

- Elk

- Horse with horseshoes

- Wild pony or horse without horseshoes

- Cow

- Goat

- Small antelope

67

ANIMALS ON THE MOVE

- Dog walking

- Dog running

- Cat walking

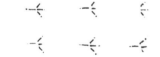

- Cat escaping and jumping on a wall

BIRDS

- Hopping birds
  (robin, sparrow, crow)

- Walking birds
  (hen, pheasant, peacock)

- Striding birds
  (stork, crane, heron)

- Water birds
  (duck, swan)

CASTING SHOE AND TIRE TRACKS

This is what you need:

- A bag of plaster
- Water
- A bowl
- A band of strong cardboard or a metal band—the kind used to bake cakes
- A few wood sticks

This is how you do it:

- Using tweezers, remove any leaves, branches, or stones that may have fallen into the shoeprint.
- Press the cardboard or metal band carefully into the soil around the print.
- Mix the plaster and pour it into the area.

Note: Plaster hardens very quickly!

- Once the plaster begins to harden, quickly push in a few wooden sticks so you can lift it more easily.
- Once the plaster is hard, carefully remove the cast and clean off the soil.

Don't forget to label it!

WHAT BIKE TRACKS REVEAL

In which direction did the man we were following ride his bike? Was he going fast or slow?

The bike tracks reveal the answers: The back tire always leaves a relatively straight track. After all, the tire is suspended on a fixed axis. The front tire, on the other hand, is suspended from the handlebars. And you surely know from your own experience that you often wobble left and right in order to keep your balance.

The more slowly you ride your bike, the stronger the wobbling gets.

The faster you ride, the easier it is to keep your balance and the loops become narrower.

This is how you determine the riding direction:

Carefully look at the loops. They always have one sharp end and one that is less sharp. The sharper end shows you the riding direction.

THE TRACK TRAP

Barbed wire functions as a magnet for tracks and other clues! If people climb over a barbed-wire fence—or merely brush against it in passing—they can easily leave tracks behind: fibers from a jacket, a small portion of their pants or a scrap of their shirt. Animals leave behind hairs from their coats.

Look for tracks on lower barbed-wire fences on hiking trails in the mountains.

Careful: If you don't want to leave any tracks yourself, be extremely careful when you climb over barbed-wire fences!

HOW TO AVOID LEAVING FOOTPRINTS

Some techniques that we have tried:
- Tie large leaves on the bottom of your shoes. They will distort your tracks a lot!
- Take a few thin branches from a bush and tie them together to form a kind of broom. Smudge your tracks with it as you go along.
- Make a track-smudging roller: Hammer many nails into a piece of wood at least 16 inches (40cm) long and 6 inches (15cm) thick. Let the nails protrude about the width of your thumb. Tie a string on the left and right ends. You can drag the roller behind you on soft soil and smudge your tracks.

Note: Naturally, you have to put down fake tracks at trail crossings.

DROP TRACKS

Certainly you've had an ice cream cone start dripping while you're eating it. Such drops can reveal a lot. They are tracks from which professionals can deduce how tall someone is or how fast someone was walking.

You can do it too. This is what different kinds of drops reveal:

Drops that have fallen from about 40 inches (1m) high

 Drops that have fallen from about 6¹/₂ feet (2m) high

Drops that have fallen from about 10 feet (3m) high

 The guy with the ice cream was walking fast and traveled in the direction of the arrow.

The guy with the ice cream was running in the direction of the arrow

 Someone was standing in one spot.

Someone was walking to the left.

 Someone was walking to the right.

OUTDOOR TIPS

THE WATCH COMPASS

When you're looking for clues outdoors, a compass can be very important. But what if you don't have a compass? You can use a regular wristwatch to determine the four directions.

This is what you need:
- A wristwatch with hands
- A thin branch or grass stem

This is what you do:
Set the watch down flat and turn it so that the hour hand points directly towards the sun. Using the grass stem, find the shortest space between the hour hand and 12 o'clock. Then divide that space in half, and that midpoint is where South is. Once you know that, it's easy to figure out what the other points of the compass are. You simply have to picture the journey the sun makes across the sky.

Another way to use nature as a compass:
The sun rises in the east and sets in the west.

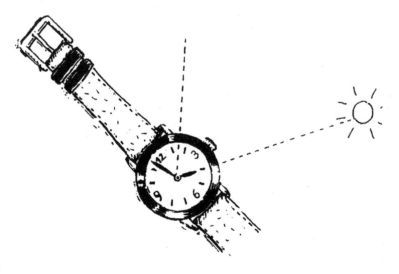

WATER FROM THE SOIL

For miles around you can't see a house, but you are terribly thirsty. What do you do?

This is what you need:
- A piece of plastic about a yard (1m) square
- A cup
- A small stone
- Many large stones
- A shovel

This is what you do:
- Dig a funnel-shaped hole in the ground—wider on top than at the bottom. It would be best to find a sun-drenched meadow for this purpose. But the soil should be slightly moist.
- Put the cup in the center of the hole.
- Put the plastic over the hole and secure it with many stones. The edges of the plastic should lie as close to the ground as possible.
- The small stone goes in the center of the plastic. Now a flat "funnel" exists, and the lowest point is directly above the cup.
- A few hours later, water will already have collected in the cup!

Why? It gets warm inside this water trap. Humidity rises from the soil and is caught by the plastic. The drops of water gather in the middle, where they fall into the cup.

EMERGENCY BACKPACK

One day Liza's backpack ended up too close to the campfire. The result was a large hole and a strong smell. How could she carry her things? Fortunately, she knew the following trick:

Take a spare pair of pants, a belt, and two pieces of rope. Tie together one leg with one of the ropes. Tie the other end of the rope to a belt loop on the pants.

Do the same thing with the second leg. Then pull the belt through the loops of the pants. Now you can use the pants as a backpack!

ALLIGATOR TIP

Dress warmly when it's hot!

Are you in a hot region, where you won't get anything to drink any time soon?

Try this: When you get water, drink as much as possible. Button up all your clothing and especially your arms and legs. Even when you get hot and sweaty, stay dressed. Keep in the shadows most of the time.

If you do this, you will not get thirsty so quickly, since your body will be able to hold in the liquid better. Have you ever noticed how inhabitants of the desert dress?

Also—take it easy and avoid any strenuous physical activity!

IF YOU GET LOST

We four have gotten lost many times.

Here are a few tips:
- Do not panic. Keep cool. Running around aimlessly does not help.
- Mark the place in which you are standing. Try to figure out where you could have lost the trail. Start tracking your trail, marking the way as you go.
- Pause from time to time and listen. Do you hear voices or dogs barking? If you do, then call for help. Don't give up!
- If you reach a hill, climb up and look for streets. Do you see smoke anywhere? Search for lights during twilight and in the dark.
- If you still have food, divide it up carefully: You don't know how long you may have to survive on it. Be especially economical with water.

THE UNSINKABLE KEY

During summer, we always tie a cork to our keys. If we lose a key in the water, it won't sink to the bottom and get lost but will float on the surface of the water.

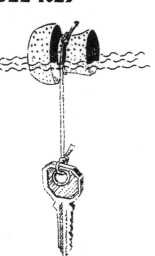

Note: Make sure the cork is big enough to keep the key afloat.

THE PANTS LIFE JACKET

A sailor once explained to us how this is done:

If your boat is sinking and you suddenly have to go overboard, immediately take off your pants in the water.

Tie the legs as tight as you can. Close the zipper and open the pants on top. Take them in both hands behind your back and throw them forward over your head. Try to fill the pants with as much air as possible—"catch" the air! Now hold the pants shut and lie down on the air-filled pants. The wetness will keep the air inside and you can rest on the pants—for a while, at least.

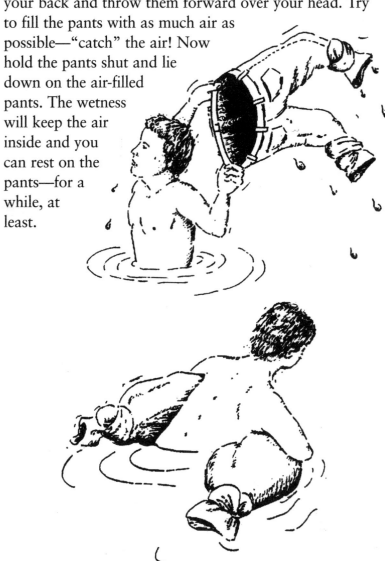

In this section you'll find some kinds of training that are also great games you can play with your friends at home.

SNEAKING INSIDE THE HOUSE

One of you has to leave the apartment or house and wait outside. Let's say it's you. In the meantime, the others prepare the house.

On an agreed-upon sign—a whistle, ringing, or yelling—you enter the house and go into the living room, bedroom, or bathroom—whichever room the group has decided on.

BUT while you are out, the others have prepared many obstacles for you, such as:

- Empty cans directly behind the door (they will rattle when you open the door)
- Strings tied across the hall or staircase, attached to bells or spoons (they will bang against each other when the string is touched)
- Aluminum foil on the ground (it rustles when stepped on)
- Chairs blocking the way

You have to get past these obstacles without making a sound. Turning on the lights or using a flashlight (torch) is not permitted.

A referee stands inside the destination room and counts all the sounds he or she can hear.

SNEAKING INTO THE YARD

This is an obstacle course. You need to creep from the starting line to the "noisy safe" and get the prize—a "valuable madness alarm clock." Of course, the prize could be anything—a pack of chewing gum, an old shoe, an empty bottle of water, or something else.

What's important is to make as little noise as possible while sneaking in. The referee stands with his or her back to the trail and raises a finger at every sound, which counts as one point. Who can manage the distance with the fewest points?

Obstacles on the Trail:
- A broomstick between two ladders. Hang lots of pot lids on it, suspended on long strings. Anyone who crawls under the broomstick and touches them is going to make noise.
- An old, large picture frame with a large piece of newspaper attached to it. You have to slit the paper open without any tools in order to climb through.
- A row of old tin cans and pots
- Crumpled newspapers
- A ladder with kitchen tools dangling from it—pots, pans, utensils, and so on. You need to climb the ladder.
- The "noisy safe" is a box with many clanking, rustling things inside. And at the very bottom lies the "valuable madness alarm clock," which is the prize. Can you lift out the treasure without making a sound?

THE GREAT ESCAPE

An Alligators game for pitch-dark nights

- Set up a start and finish line in a field.
- The watchman stands on the finish line.
- You—the prisoner—stand on the starting line. Your goal is to escape.
- You make your escape by creeping up to the finish line without making a sound.
- If the watchman hears anything, he calls "STOP!" and you are not allowed to move any more.
- The watchman points his flashlight in the direction of the sound and turns it on. If the light hits you, you've been captured.

WHO DID IT?

The Fingerprint Game

Four or more people can play this game.

You'll need equipment for making fingerprints. The first thing you do is make a fingerprint card for each one of the players.

Then you need a bottle. Wipe it off carefully with a towel to remove all fingerprints.

Now one player leaves the room. Let's say that's you. You are the Detective. While you are out of the room, someone grabs the bottle, puts it back down, and sits down again.

You come back in and take off the fingerprint with whatever powder you're using. You compare the fingerprint with those on the individual cards. If you find the "culprit," you win. The culprit becomes the new Detective.

THRILLER QUESTIONS

Did you read all the chapters and memorize the techniques and tips? Great—now you can start the Detective Test. You get 40 questions. Find the right answers and write them in your notebook.

Once you've answered all the questions, check out the solutions. For every correct answer, you get one point. Add your points. On page 94, you'll get your test results.

If you didn't do too well, don't worry. Read the book again and take the test again. You'll definitely improve!

We'll keep our fingers crossed.

❊   ❊   ❊

1. Alex gives you this sign under-water.
Thriller Question: What does it mean?

2. Carlos brought in his detective suitcase. It contained the following items:

- A magnifying glass
- A strong flashlight
- A camera
- A pen and pencil
- Coins for phone calls
- Large pieces of paper
- A small scissors
- Tweezers
- A tape measure
- Rubber gloves

Thriller Question: How many things are missing?

3. Alex is gasping for breath. He has followed a suspect across town and into an office building. Annoyingly, the man has disappeared into an unmarked office with a door of frosted glass.

Thriller Question: What does Alex have to do in order to see what is going on through the glass?

4. Poppy is approaching you, but doesn't know you. Her index finger is shaking.

Thriller Question: Is Poppy sick?

5.

Thriller Question: What is this spy telling you?

6.

Thriller Question: Can you lift this glass without touching the outside?

7.

Thriller Question: Did someone search these documents?

8.

Thriller Question: From what height did this drop? From 40 inches (1m)? 6½ feet (2m)? or 10 feet (3m)?

9. Liza is in a forest. Suddenly she sends you a blink sign. She quickly moves her flashlight back and forth.

Thriller Question: What does this mean?

0. You discover two footprints. They come from the ne person who wore the same shoes in both cases. wards the house, the prints are flatter, towards the street, they are deeper.

Thriller Question: What can you deduce from this?

11. This is a secret letter. It was written in water writing.

Thriller Question: What do you do with it?

12.

Thriller Question: In what direction did the bike go?

13. You know that an incriminating letter is in the suspect's desk drawer. You want to read it, but you don't want to leave any fingerprints.

Thriller Question: How do you open the drawer if you've forgotten your gloves?

14. Imagine that you're flying over an area in which a plane has crashed. Suddenly, you see a sign, made from stones, emerge on the ground.

Thriller Question: What does this sign mean?

15. Carlos wants to get rid of the person who has been following him for an hour. He walks into a large office building and asks the receptionist a question.

Thriller Question: What did he ask?

16.
Thriller Question: Which footprint comes from an old shoe and which comes from a new one?

17. You can only see the suspect's eyes as small black dots.
Thriller Question: How far away is the person?

18.
Thriller Question: Did this bike go fast or slow?

19. You get a harmless-looking letter from your buddy. Nothing is written with secret ink and there is no water writing on the paper.
Thriller Question: Where will you find the secret message?

20.
Thriller Question: Did someone enter this room?

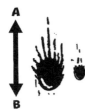

21. The thief calmly licked the ice cream when suddenly the Alligators appeared behind him. He ran away as fast as he could.
Thriller Question: Which way did he run?

22. Liza comes to you and says, "Can you please tell me what time it is? My watch stopped at 2 p.m."
Thriller Question: What does this message mean?

23. You find a box in Poppy's room that contains a secret diary and many messages. It stands closed between

some books, so that anybody could find it right away.
Thriller Question: Did Poppy forget to put it away?

24.
Thriller Question: What does this track tell you?

25. Liza is being followed. She wants to get a good look at the person who is trailing her, but she doesn't want to turn around. That would be too obvious and would tell the pursuer that she had seen him. She doesn't have a mirror with her. Then she walks into the mall.
Thriller Question: What is she going to do?

26. These things are written on Poppy's people card.
• Name   • Phone number
• Height   • Weight
• Birth date • Zodiac sign
• Likes a lot • Does not like
• Notes
Thriller Question: What is missing?

27. Alex's pursuers are puzzled. They followed his tracks and have arrived at a cliff. There the ground falls steeply 60 feet (18m) into the roaring sea.
Thriller Question: What did Alex do?

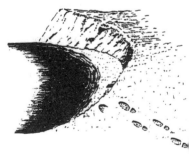

28.
Thriller Question: What mistake is this detective making?

29. Finally the Alligators caught sight of the suspect. "Come on, let's trail him," said Carlos.
Thriller Question: What did the Alligators do?

30.
Thriller Question: What animal left these tracks?

31. Poppy got a new secret camera. On the way home, she got a suitable shoebox right away. As soon as the secret camera was ready, she started taking photographs. Her father didn't realize that she was taking a picture of him. But Poppy was very disappointed with the pictures. The only thing you could see was a shoe.
Thriller Question: What did Poppy do wrong?

32.
Thriller Question: What does this tramp sign mean?

33. Only one fingerprint really matches that of Carlos. There are two marks that prove it.
Thriller Question: Which print is it?

| 1 | 2 | 3 | 4 | 5 |

34. You're in the Sahara Desert. It's terribly hot and your water supplies are dwindling fast.
Thriller Question: What should you do about your clothes?

35. You get a message with many letters that do not make sense.

Thriller Question: What do you need in order to decode the message from left to right?

 36.
Thriller Question: What does this marking mean?

37.
Thriller Question: What does this cat track tell you?

38.

Thriller Question: Can you lip-read? What three words is this woman saying?

- My new car
- Tomorrow at eight
- Don't kid me.
- I killed him.

39.

Thriller Question: What is Carlos telling his friend?

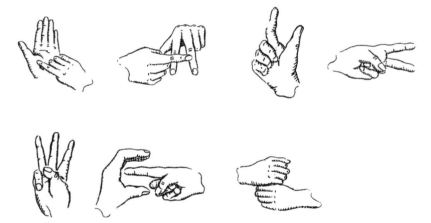

40.

Thriller Question: What do you need in order to make an emergency backpack?

Answers start on page 92. For every correct answer you get one point. Then check page 94 for your test results.

THRILLER ANSWERS

1. Thriller Answer: I am running out of air!

2. Thriller Answer: 5—the notepad, fingerprint powder, envelopes, chalk, and whistle.

3. Thriller Answer: Press a piece of tape against the glass.

4. Thriller Answer: No, she's scared. Someone is probably following her.

5. Thriller Answer: No one must realize that we are together.

6. Thriller Answer: Yes, stick your fingers inside the glass and spread them.

7. Thriller Answer: Yes, the zigzag line on the side reveals it.

8. Thriller Answer: From the height of $6^{1}/_{2}$ feet (2m).

9. Thriller Answer: Help!

10. Thriller Answer: The person carried something heavy from the house.

11. Thriller Answer: Dip the paper in water.

12. Thriller Answer: To the right.

13. Thriller Answer: With one or two pencils.

14. Thriller Answer: Everything is all right.

15. Thriller Answer: For the back entrance.

16. Thriller Answer: Print A is from an old shoe. Print B is from a new one.

17. Thriller Answer: About 330 feet (100m).

18. Thriller Answer: Fast.

19. Thriller Answer: Behind the stamp.

20. Thriller Answer: Yes, the paper was moved when the door was opened.

21. Thriller Answer: To A.

22. Thriller Answer: Meeting at 2:00.

23. Thriller Answer: No, the box is just meant to distract from the real hiding place.

24. Thriller Answer: The suspect is walking with a stick or cane.

25. Thriller Answer: Stand in front of a shop window and use it as a giant mirror.

26. Thriller Answer: Three points: age, address, distinguishing marks.

27. Thriller Answer: Left a fake trail by walking backwards.

28. Thriller Answer: Everyone can see that he's not reading the newspaper. It's too close to his face.

29. Thriller Answer: They split up and only one of them shadowed the suspect.

30. Thriller Answer: A horse or pony without horseshoes.

31. Thriller Answer: She didn't practice.

32. Thriller Answer: Attention! Danger!

33. Thriller Answer: Fingerprint #3.

34. Thriller Answer: Button them up. Definitely don't take anything off.

35. Thriller Answer: A ruler.

36. Thriller Answer: Careful—dog bites!

37. Thriller Answer: The cat fled and jumped on the wall.

38. Thriller Answer: My new car.

39. Thriller Answer: Run away!

40. Thriller Answer: A pair of pants, two pieces of rope, and a belt.

TEST RESULTS

Did you give yourself one point for each correct answer? Then add them up and see how well you did in the Great Alligator Detective Test. How did you do? We're curious, aren't you?

1–6 Beginner

7–12 Student

13–20 Trainee

21–27 Hobbyist

28–34 Junior Detective

35–40 Pro

INDEX